ideals
AUTUMN

There is a charm in autumn's wine-sweet days
Not to be found in any other time.
Her golden bounty satisfies the gaze
And stirs the heart to reveries sublime.
For now is born the reason for the spring—
Fruition of the seed and of the mind—
When autumn proves the good of everything,
And all the doubt of youth is left behind.
The flaming trees against a sapphire sky,
The heaped-up harvest of the mellow land,
Together they spell wealth no gold can buy,
That only heart and soul can understand.
Each season answers Nature's every need,
But autumn keeps the promise of the seed.

Elizabeth Ann M. Moore

ISBN 0-8249-1005-2 350

IDEALS—Vol. 38, No. 6 September MCMLXXXI. IDEALS (ISSN 0019-137X) is published eight times a year,
January, February, April, June, July, September, October, November
by IDEALS PUBLISHING CORPORATION, 11315 Watertown Plank Road, Milwaukee, Wis. 53226
Second class postage paid at Milwaukee, Wisconsin. Copyright © MCMLXXXI by IDEALS PUBLISHING CORPORATION.
Postmaster, please send form 3579 to Ideals Publishing Corporation, Post Office Box 2100, Milwaukee, Wis. 53201
All rights reserved. Title IDEALS registered U.S. Patent Office.
Published simultaneously in Canada.

ONE-YEAR SUBSCRIPTION—eight consecutive issues as published—$15.95
TWO-YEAR SUBSCRIPTION—sixteen consecutive issues as published—$27.95
SINGLE ISSUES—$3.50

Publisher, James A. Kuse
Managing Editor, Ralph Luedtke
Editor/Ideals, Colleen Callahan Gonring
Associate Editor, Linda Robinson
Production Manager, Mark Brunner
Photographic Editor, Gerald Koser
Copy Editor, Barbara Nevid
Art Editor, Duane Weaver

Month of Dreams

Dixie R. Danielson

Myriad colored leaves tumble
Slowly to the ground.
Fluffy deep-piled clouds, where
The dreams of youth abound;
Gentle breezes blowing,
Caressing sun-warmed sands;
Dusty hills and mountains rest
In soothing Autumn's hands.
Along the peaceful river banks
Droop lightly napping willows,
Trailing slender branches
In foamy liquid pillows.
Serenely, hawks with wings outspread
Glide smoothly through the air,
While I know warm September dreams,
This autumn day so fair.

Autumn Symphony

Catherine E. Jackson

Summer's end is a symphony,
A lyric in color—a rhapsody.
The myriad tones are Nature's rendition
Of an old refrain in a new composition.
Though amber and gold set a waltz-time tempo,
A touch of scarlet has forced crescendo.
Here the brown foliage is trying a dirge,
A farewell to summer, so fall may emerge.
The dainty ballet of a falling leaf
Is attempting a change to a lighter motif;
The waning breeze hums a soft innuendo
To the plaintive cry of a lonely swallow.
In the hazy distance there's a muted murmur,
The dulcet tones of departed summer.

When Autumn Comes

Garnett Ann Schultz

Oh, splendor of the universe
When spring and summer run their course,
God dips His paintbrush slowly in,
For autumn is the work of Him.

The brilliant sumac, scarlet there,
The gorgeous sunset, none compare,
The hills are splashed in gold and brown,
While leaves of saffron tumble down.

Oh, world of crimson, golden hue,
Just nothing can compare with you.
Most lovely time of all the year,
When autumn comes to bless us here.

My soul enriched, I watch it all,
The blessings of the gorgeous fall—
The rain splashed hills, then golden suns,
A smiling world—when autumn comes.

Country Lane

Haydn S. Pearson

A country lane is one of the most appealing of nature's pictures. It is homey and intimate. It does not have the grandeur of ledge-topped mountains nor the sweep of evergreen hillsides. But somehow man frequently appreciates the small and familiar more than he does the grand and awesome.

A country lane is not a public way. It is a private, personal path or road. You see lanes leading from barnyards to pastures; they branch from dirt roads and lead across fields and meadows. They climb pasture hillsides to maple sugar groves and to woodlots on the slope.

Now the walls and fences resemble gray stitching on the landscape. The birches, alders, hornbeams, and sumacs are feathery; birds' nests are wind-torn blotches. The gray paper cones of hornets' nests swing at the tips of supple branches. Goldenrod heads are gray and bleached, and tall stalks of mullein stand above frost-brown grasses.

Walk a country lane on a golden day in October. Away from the sound of traffic, a man can feel the assurance that a peaceful environment brings. He can enjoy that poignant period in the fall when the countryside is again revealed after the hardwoods and shrubs have dropped their leaves.

Reprinted from THE NEW ENGLAND YEAR by Haydn S. Pearson, with the permission of W. W. Norton & Company, Inc. Copyright © 1966 by W. W. Norton & Company, Inc.

A Labor Day Gift

Carole Joyce Davis

My gaze rests fondly on the beautiful shade tree that keeps a leafy awning hoisted over our front yard during the spring and summer months.

It is autumn now and the leaves will soon turn a brilliant red. Each leaf will tumble down in a colorful blaze of glory, like a noiseless exploding skyrocket, its mission accomplished for another year. With the winter comes rest and a different kind of beauty, as stark and barren branches become shelves for snow and havens for wintering birds.

Over the years the tree has grown tall and sturdy. In the spring we follow the magnificent process of buds-to-blossoms. Hundreds of pink flowers, each with its quintet of petals, burst forth in glorious profusion, reminding us once again of what a splendid gift choice was this tree.

It is really my husband's tree, you see, having been a special gift to him from four special children. It is that rare and wonderful kind of gift that continues to bring pleasure long after the actual event which, in this case, was fifteen years ago.

That was the year my husband's birthday and Labor Day happened to coincide, and the children decided their hardworking Dad definitely deserved an unusual present. This posed quite a challenge to them: to think of *one* gift from the *four* of them to cover *two* celebrations that fell on the *same* day!

Several whispered conferences failed to produce a single idea they all agreed on. One by one each suggestion was vetoed with a "Naw, that's no good." September approached and no decision had been reached.

There were many other things going on at this same time. The lazy days of summer, filled with picnics and swimming, would end abruptly when we reached the circled date on the calendar denoting that all-important first day of school. We had also moved during the summer and were still getting ourselves settled into a brand-new home.

The decision of what to give Dad, however, was made for us after a particularly violent rainstorm. Much as we enjoyed our new surroundings, the one thing sadly lacking was adequate planting.

Breathlessly I listened to them. They were just one vote away from an almost unheard of phenomenon—total unanimity! One more voice to be heard, from the youngest (aged four). Would she agree?

"Can they be pink flowers?" she asked eagerly.

And so it was settled. We found just the right tree and presented it along with a shiny new wheelbarrow to Dad on his special day that year. He planted it exactly where his four precious imps directed, by the brick front walk.

By the following year the young tree had taken hold and affirmed its place solidly in the earth. The children were pleased with their gift and so was their Dad.

During those busy and often hectic growing-up years, each achievement and each proud moment by each child seemed to be accompanied by a new pink blossom on the tree. They grew together. As the children began to branch out in their interests and abilities so did the tree begin to send tall branches skyward. Both the tree and the children began to flex their limbs and occasionally stretched them too far. A wound to the ego was just as shattering as when a harsh winter's freezing rain snapped off a too-long branch.

The trunk on the tree became sturdier and stronger. We too became more and more capable of withstanding the shocks, bumps, and prunings that are a part of life. No winds from either Mother Nature or misfortune have been great enough to knock down that tree or any of us. We too have affirmed our place solidly on this earth.

The children have all left home now, and that's exactly as it should be. The tree has indeed grown "high, high up" as well as having spread over a wide area of our front yard. We know that the children, like the tree, have also spread themselves to new areas to cast their own special knowledge and talents upon the world.

We've had several new pink blossoms lately, not only on the tree but in our lives as well. Promotions and advancements in life are reflected by added blooms on the tree. We've also seen some petals fall too early. Sorrows and disappointments often cause petals and tears to fall together.

The cycle goes on. A closer look today reveals a few leaves tinged with red after all. In a week or two the Labor Day Birthday tree will explode again into a spectacular crimson red color. If those dark clouds gathering overhead mean rain, then the tape recorder in my mind will click on again, and I can once again hear a small voice excitedly call out, "Let's get Daddy a tree . . ."

We'd managed to get a good start on a lawn, but when it rained hard there were several "squishy" places in the front yard, especially by the brick walk. Eventually we would need to plant trees or shrubs in these low spots.

"That's it!" our eldest (aged ten) shouted, running outside when the rain had stopped. "Let's get Daddy a tree for his birthday and Labor Day. Let's plant it right *here*," she said, stamping her feet on the soggy lawn.

"Hey, that's a great idea," agreed the second (aged eight). "It's too muddy out here anyhow. We need a tree in our yard, one that has pretty flowers."

"A big tree," said the third (aged six). "One that grows high, high up and will give lots of shade."

Autumn Laughter

Like gay laughter in the sun,
Down the leaves come one by one;
From the maple red they fall;
Frosty North Wind kissed them all.

Elms in yellow, oak trees brown,
See the leaves come tumbling down;
Flaming sumac, goldenrod,
Make the heart feel close to God.

Jack Frost brushed the fields in white,
And the blackbird's song is bright
On his way to sunny clime,
Ahead of cold and wintertime.

Children's laughter rings out, too,
Under skies October blue,
As they run and laugh and play;
Old King Winter's on his way.

Annette Wildman Swearingen

Autumn's Jewels

How gay they seem and rightly so,
For they are all arrayed
In raiment of such vivid hue,
Their glory is displayed.

'Tis raining leaves of red and gold
Upon the earth today;
They tumble, twist and flit about
As children in their play.

The rush of frost upon the green
Brought forth their inner glow,
A deeply mirrored reflection
Of summer's last rainbow.

As chilling breezes loose their hold
And snatch them from the trees,
The earth is richly carpeted
With autumn's jeweled leaves.

Wilma Willett Fuchs

Nature's Parade

Wyatt Cullom

There is a nip in the early morning air. The sky has put on a deeper tone of blue. I watch the hawk as he soars upward in effortless flight. Higher and higher he spirals until the tiny speck is swallowed into the void of infinity. I turn my eyes toward a honking chevron of wild geese spearheading southward. With no maps, sexton or compass to direct them, they travel unerringly to faraway sanctuaries and havens in the tropics.

The trees will soon shed their garments of green, but first there must be a parade. Their garments must be transformed into hues of golden yellow, red and russet brown. Nature's parade becomes a color spectacular, as the trees bask in the autumn sunlight. Finally the leaves begin to lose their grip, as the brisk north winds moan among their timely branches. How pathetic that they must shed their robes when they have reached their peak of beauty.

The balmy days of autumn have even another colorful spectacle in store. Just turn your eyes toward the western horizon when the sun is descending. Across the canvas of the western skies, God begins to paint the clouds with glowing colors. We behold the spacious dome; slowly it is transformed into flames of living fire, ever changing from greenish gold to brilliant red, yellow and orange. Then from the peak of its blazing glory, it slowly fades into the twilight, as another day makes its exit in a riot of splendor.

September

Harmony Schupp

Golden is September's sun,
    And purple is the haze
Veiling distant horizons
    These glorious autumn days.

Purple are the clustered grapes,
    And gold the Bartlett pear.
Golden is the new fall dress
    The maple tree will wear.

Golden is the hickory grove
    Down by the woodsy lane.
Purple are the high-piled clouds
    That indicate a rain.

Purple are the asters wild
    That by the millstream nod.
Golden are the butterflies,
    Marigolds and goldenrod.

Purple are alfalfa blooms;
    Last cutting time is nigh.
Golden is the ripening corn,
    And gold is pumpkin pie.

Gold and purple, queens adorn,
    And monarchs call their due.
September flaunts these gaudy hues,
    For she is royal, too.

Transition

Dorothy Evelyn Begg

The sumac fires are kindling now
Upon the green hill's distant brow.

Bright berries of the elder shine
By cool wild grapes on tendriled vine.

Sweet fern spices the roadside air
Where grazing cows in wonder stare.

The honeysuckle's yellow sweet
Quickens the wild bee's small heartbeat.

Field mice eye the milkweed pod
Fattening midst the goldenrod.

Queen Anne's lace and clover red
Make the young foal's fragrant bed.

Summer's heart is smoking fire
Ringing round the pasture mire.

Soon the flames will reach the trees
And burst in autumn symphonies!

September

Emilee Hines

September is a rich, full-bodied month.
It's fields of new-cut hay drying fragrant in the sun,
Trees hanging heavy with amber-colored pears,
Cicada calls at night and dewdrop-
spangled spider webs at dawn.

September is a royal month,
Moving by at leisurely, majestic pace,
Clad in deep purple ironweed and stately goldenrod,
With brown-eyed Susans freckled on its face.

September is a time for looking back to summer,
Somehow gone without a trace,
To past Septembers when we were young,
Our schoolbooks new and our dreams
as yet uncompromised.

September is a slightly sleepy afternoon
Spent talking, shelling peas, sitting in the swing,
Being glad it's not so hot today
And maybe the grass won't have to
be cut again this year.

September is summer's last burst of harvest
And a hint of winter's coming sleep.

Time Bends
the Bough

Fern M. Impola

Autumn holds fulfillment in her hand;
Against the hemlocks' jasmine tapestry,
The flame of oak is bright across the land.
The seeds of spring have gained maturity;
No longer do they grope through portals, dark
Beneath the ground; a striving toward the light
Arrayed them in a brillant sphere, where lark
And wren embrace the air in joyous flight.

But tares and wheat stand side by side, the length
And breadth of earth, and thorns infest the rose.
Beyond all human force a master strength
Will nourish every fragile stalk that grows.
Fulfillment comes—time bends the laden bough,
And fields are ripe unto the harvest now.

The Wheat Is Turning

Minnie Klemme

The wheat is turning
From green to burnished gold.
It will be cut and harvested
Before the month is old.

Sown in September,
It grew and flourished, then
Lay dormant under winter snow
To green and grow again.

Now seed and sower
In summer's harvest meet,
And there is straw for storage,
And there is bread to eat.

North Woods Notebook

Butchering Hogs, Digging Bulbs, and Choking the Herring

My husband, Bob, was the youngest of ten children born to Comb and Anna Andersen Bourgeois. The family lived in Park Falls, Wisconsin, when Bob was born on August 20, 1923; during his childhood there were several moves to farms and small towns throughout northern Wisconsin.

Bob's memories of his childhood remain vivid. When he talks about those distant days, the memories come alive; they are echoes of a way of life that has all but disappeared from the American scene.

Bea Bourgeois

Getting ready for winter on the farm meant a lot of work for all of us. We had a huge garden because there were so many of us to feed; so the carrots, rutabagas, and turnips all had to be dug up and brought into the basement for winter storage. My brothers Milt and Ed and I helped pick hundreds of apples and wrapped each one in newspaper; they were separated by varieties—Wealthies and Greenings were the hardiest and would keep in their barrels well into the middle of winter. It's nothing now to have fresh fruit the year round, but in those days nothing tasted finer than a fresh apple in mid-January.

I remember that after all the Hubbard squash was gathered, we stored it underneath our beds where it was warm and dry. We picked pumpkins in the fall, too; so the kids would carve Jack-o'-lanterns at Halloween, and so that Ma could can the pumpkin meat for pies.

Ma always had a gorgeous flower garden, but the gladiolus were her favorites. She spent years trying to come up with new colors by hybridizing, and as a result there were a lot of bulbs to dig out every fall. We marked them according to color and stored them in the basement.

During my high school years, 1937 to 1941, I worked on a neighbor's farm cutting corn by hand for silage. We'd start in late September, and we used a large sharp knife like a machete. We cut the stalks off close to the ground and piled them in shocks to be picked up by a horse-drawn wagon. The stalks were taken to a cutting machine that chewed up everything and shot the ground corn into the silo. Dad used to tell me that as the corn fermented in the silo, the pigs would eat from the bottom and get drunk. Somehow I think that was one of his better fables.

The onset of cold weather always meant that butchering would be on the schedule. We waited for the first snow so the meat would freeze and not spoil. Pa would stick the pigs in the neck to kill them; then, because nobody else wanted the job, I had to catch the blood in a large pan, mix it with salt, and keep it cold while I stirred it so that it wouldn't clot, and Ma could use it for blood sausage.

During the fall of my junior and senior years, I worked at the fish docks in Cornucopia during the herring run, which peaked about Thanksgiving time. On weekends and over the Thanksgiving vacation, I would go out on Lake Superior with the commercial fishermen, who depended on a good herring run to provide the money that would support them and their families through the winter.

I remember the biting cold on the lake, even though we wore heavy clothing and oilers to keep us dry. I also remember the foul odor of the bilge in the boat and the smell of the coal stove; some days the lake was so rough that the waves would wash over the top, into the stove's chimney, and onto the coal. It made an obnoxious odor that seemed to permeate everything.

The herring nets were about four feet wide and almost a half-mile long. They were tremendously heavy when they were full of fish; so there was a mechanical net lifter on board to haul them in. After they were emptied, the nets had to be stacked precisely in net boxes at the back of the boat so they'd be ready for the next day's fishing. My sister Irene's husband, Walt Lawin, would stand on the unprotected, slippery deck wrestling with those nets to make sure there were no knots or twists in them as they were stacked.

Sometimes we had a little unintentional comic relief on board. I remember once an old Russian man named Chernowski was fishing with us, and we had taken in a huge haul of herring. Chernowski happened to wear false teeth, and in the rush of unloading the net, his dentures dropped out into the pile of slippery fish. He simply picked them up, shook them off, and popped them back into his mouth. It was a sight I've never forgotten.

One of my jobs was to "choke" the herring that were caught in the openings in the nets. The fishermen used gill nets, which caught the herring by their gills; as the nets were pulled on board, we "choked" the herring through by twisting their heads and pulling them out of the nets.

After we had filled all the boxes on board with herring, they were taken to the fish sheds in Cornuco-

pia. The fishermen's wives and other women who were available to work would gut the fish, wash them, and pack them in salt, so they could be trucked to processing plants. The men would scoop tons of fresh herring out of the boxes and throw them onto long tables where the women stood ready to work. About twenty women were lined up at the tables, and each station had two boards in a V-shape over a hole in the table underneath where the entrails fell through into buckets. Nothing was wasted; the innards were used as fertilizer on many farms near Cornie.

Whether it would be a good Christmas or a bad Christmas depended a lot on the herring run, and some years were better than others. There was competition among the women who worked in the fish sheds, because they were paid by the box. Some could work

faster than others, and there was a great explosion if a fast worker ran out of fish to gut and clean.

During the herring season, Poncho's Bar in Cornucopia was a favorite gathering place at the end of the day. I remember that the whole tavern smelled like fish, and you could walk in any time and find fish scales stuck to the long mahogany bar and to the sleeves of every fisherman's jacket.

I graduated from high school in June of 1941 and worked that following fall on the herring run. We would go out at six o'clock in the morning and return to shore about six o'clock at night.

We had gone out on Sunday, December seventh, as always. I don't think any one of us was prepared for the shattering news we heard as soon as we got off the boats on that sad, historic night.

October on the Farm

Agnes Davenport Bond

The skies are soft with fleeting clouds,
This fresh October day;
And gorgeous-colored shrubs and trees
Make hills and valleys gay.

A roving brooklet winds about
And here and there is seen,
With cattle grazing near its banks,
Where meadows still are green.

The scraggly boughs still hang with fruit
Upon the apple trees;
And leaves are dancing in the air
With every gentle breeze.

The peaceful sheep, in fleecy coats,
Are browsing on the hill;
And in the barnyard, cackling hens
Are roaming round at will.

The golden pumpkins, big and round,
Their wilted vines adorn
And brighten up the somber field
Of faded shocks of corn.

The frosty, early-morning air,
The changing winds that blow
Are true reminders of the fact
That fall days soon must go.

The showy leaves, all red and gold,
Must soon be brown and dry;
And naked trees, like sentinels,
Will stand against the sky.

So while we scuff in fallen leaves,
Which rustle neath our feet,
We know that they forebode the time
When fall and winter meet.

God's Gift

Russell T. Brown

I talked with God just yesterday
　For it was early spring;
I watched His green world come to life—
　A most inspiring thing.

　　I walked with Him through summer
　　　And watched the whole world grow;
　　I basked in summer's sunshine
　　　And prayed 'twould never go.

　　　　But I awoke this morning,
　　　　　And autumn filled the air;
　　　　The green leaves turned to crimson,
　　　　　And God was everywhere.

I strolled through field and woodland,
　Ablaze on every knoll,
A preview of God's heaven;
　Its beauty filled my soul.

　　Tomorrow will be winter,
　　　And God will still be there;
　　But I'm sure He sent me autumn,
　　　His jeweled gift to share.

When Autumn Leaves Are Browned

After autumn's brilliant colors
    And the leaves have all been browned,
And beneath the trees in woodlands,
    They have covered deep the ground;
While there's still a touch of orange
    In the tangled bittersweet,
There's music in those dry brown leaves
    That rustle round your feet.

When each morning, cool and chilly,
    Shows a covering of frost,
And the brown leaves lie in waiting
    For a chance to be wind-tossed,
There's something about the weather then
    That quickens up the step,
Puts new life into every vein
    And fills you full of pep.

Wild geese in wedge formation
    Are oft seen winging by,
Sometimes a faint line waving
    Like a ribbon in the sky.
The little grove all summer hid
    Is now exposed to view,
Where a fruit so rich and luscious,
    The Hoosier papaw, grew.

Smoke curling from the chimneys
    Adds a touch more beautified,
Where the houses dot the landscape
    Throughout the countryside.
To me there comes a feeling,
    Makes me want to tramp around
O'er hills and valleys, woods and fields,
    When autumn leaves are browned.

Ottis Shirk

The Frost This Morning

The frost this morning spread itself
Like diamonds on the land;
It rested on the turning leaves
That blushed with colors grand.

I saw the pumpkins in the fields,
The corn shocks standing by;
The morning sun had risen, too,
So blue was yonder sky.

Chrysanthemums in gold and rust
Adorned the garden, too;
The apples in the orchard spoke
Of autumn's magic hue.

I love this time of year, I do,
When tangy is the air;
And hiking down the forest paths
Brings views beyond compare.

Georgia B. Adams

When Autumn Comes to Call

We've a welcome, warm and friendly,
For the very first days of fall,
When the ripening fields are fragrant and sweet
Beyond the pasture wall,
When fleecy white clouds are high and adrift
In a beautiful sea of blue,
And faraway hills are wrapped in the glow
Of the everchanging hues.

We've a greeting, gay and cordial,
When Autumn comes to call,
When the mountain trails are beckoning
And leaves begin to fall,
When merriment rings from children at play
Until the school bell tolls,
When hovering clouds bring a promise of rain
And a sky of parasols.

We've a feeling of joy and wonder
When the earth is etched in white,
When the delicate boughs are bending with frost,
Aglow in the dawning light,
When meadow and field wear a shimmering gown
And woodsmoke curls through the grove,
When crickets all cease their singing and drowse
In the silence, crisp and cold.

We've a feeling of deep contentment
When the silo and bins are filled,
When the poplars fling their shower of gold
And a brown leaf lingers still.
We've a welcome, warm and friendly,
When Autumn comes to call;
Then our hearts can sing of beautiful hills
And the loveliest days of all!

Joy Belle Burgess

Autumn's Artwork

Louise Weibert Sutton

Clear and crisp, the days of harvest,
As red leaves begin to fly,
Spread in breezy autumn splendor
Underneath a matchless sky.
Now that summer's heat has embered,
Great chrysanthemums, like gold,
Spend their coin of yellow treasure
As the perfect days unfold.

Warm-lit fires on chilly evenings
Bless our homes and hearths once more,
As, outside, fall's leafy dancers
Swirl across earth's browning floor.
All along each country roadside,
Sporting apple, quince or pear,
Pleasant smells of autumn mingle
Fruity fragrance everywhere.

Rounding slowly through the twilight
Comes a big October moon
Over silhouetted valleys
To an old owl's plaintive tune.
Halloween and then Thanksgiving
Soon will form their special part
Of the precious joys of living
Close to autumn's friendly heart!

Golden Harvest

Autumn's golden beauty shineth
O'er the land in full array.
Barns are almost bursting over,
Brimming full of sweet dry hay.

Velvet skies of autumn evenings
Hold a mellow harvest moon—
Just a silent, sweet reminder
That she'll leave us all too soon.

Autumn's wealth of golden harvest
Lays her bounty at our door—
Gifts of nature's rich fulfillment
Proving God's abundant store.

Carice Williams

Come Walk with Me

Come walk with me along the country lanes
As Autumn weaves her brilliant tapestries;
No mortal hand could blend such vivid dyes
Nor drape the woods in mantles such as these.

Where else but here on sun-drenched rolling hills
Where woodsmoke rises on the frosty air
Can we discover vistas quite so bright,
Or valleys quite so charming or so fair?

Let's saunter slowly down a woodland trail
Or take a rambling road to who-knows-where,
With fences hung with orange bittersweet
And crimson woodbine dangling everywhere.

We'll smell the pungent tang of pennyroyal,
Of pawpaws and persimmons in the sun;
We'll revel in the beauty of the glades
And wander through the hills till day is done.

And later, as the evening shadows fall
With sunlight slowly fading in the west,
We then shall turn and seek the homeward trail
As twilight calls us back to home, and rest.

Mina Morris Scott

Autumn Tapestry

Special Thoughts about Autumn

No spring nor summer beauty hath such grace,
As I have seen in one autumnal face.

John Donne

Autumn Benediction

The autumn bird
Sings his prayer of peace,
As man and field their labors cease;
God in His Heaven nods His praise
In warm benediction of autumn days.

Margaret Freer

The Kind Earth

Earth is here so kind,
That just tickle her with a hoe,
And she laughs with a harvest.

Douglas Jerrold

Autumn's Coming

September—and a longer shadow falls
From slanted sunbeams; and the blue jay calls
Insistently. The purple-fruited vines
Show age-brown leaves while all the mystic signs
That herald autumn's coming now appear.

Ruth Winslow Gordon

Autumn

A shower of brown from a wind-tossed tree,
A ripple of red like a painted sea,
Children with rakes, and leaves flying free—
Autumn is here again!

Mary E. Richardson

By all these lovely tokens
September days are here,
With summer's best of weather
And autumn's best of cheer.

Helen Hunt Jackson

September

Butter-soft and mellow September treads in
With a bar of golden yellow in her hair.

Glenna James

Autumn Prayer

Bring the glory of autumn into our souls,
The peace of God to our hearts.
We bow our heads in reverent grace
For the blessings this season imparts.

Vera Stahly

The Vintage Years

A lovely Indian summer day,
The golden hours soon slip away.
The evening haze that's everywhere,
A touch of frost that's in the air,
These are the days, sweet as aged wine—
These treasured days—
Life's autumntime.

Gladys Gould Noll

October

First frost tonight,
Stars wink winter warning;
Yet, warm is the kiss
Of autumn's golden morning.

Betty Hunter

Autumn Beauty

A lovely picture for famished eyes
Gazing at meadows and autumn skies,
We enjoy God's gifts, created for all,
As we drink in beauty of early fall.

Lucille Sahakian

Autumn

When Autumn blends her colors
In a panoramic view
Over fields, woods and hillsides
In variegated hue,
We stand and gaze in wonder
At the lavishness arrayed
In the beauty and the vastness
Of God's handiwork displayed.

Ottis Shirk

You cannot hope to enjoy the harvest
Without laboring in the field.

Plaque

Harvest Beauty

The harvest's golden beauty,
Burnished bright,
Shines forth across a great
And growing land;
Shines out in radiance and in love
From the face of man.

Elizabeth Searle Lamb

Magic

I love the way that Autumn trims a town,
September-kissed,
With russet lace and furbelows of brown
And violet mist.
I love the way her hands can touch a tree
And leave a trace
Of gold dust and of scarlet witchery
Upon its face.

Catherine E. Berry

October Music

Wild geese are notes of music
Penciled across the sky,
The poignant orchestration
Of summer's farewell cry.

Ruth Garrison Scurlock

ONE PRECIOUS HOUR

One autumn day I spent an hour
Just sitting in the morning sun.
I drank in all the beauty there,
Declaring summer's work was done.

I watched the soft white clouds appear
Like powder puffs in azure sky;
I saw them float with grace supreme
As if to say a sweet good-bye.

While I was sitting in the sun,
I saw the wild geese overhead;
As they flew southward with the clouds,
I saw a maple leaf turn red.

I watched the walnut leaves come down,
Some swiftly flying round and round,
And when I turned my head away,
I heard a walnut hit the ground.

High in an apple tree nearby
Red apples proudly gave display,
Awaiting tender hands to come
And lay them carefully away.

The gourds that on the trellis clung
Showed brightly there and pleased the eye;
A pumpkin, like a pot of gold,
Lay in a garden spot nearby.

If I had had another hour to sit
There in the autumn sun,
I know my heart could not have held
The joy I found as, one by one,

The acts of splendor passed along
In gay parade of autumn grace,
The grandeur of the season's spell
Which makes the world a sweeter place.

Eleanor T. Drake

Autumn's Vital Signs

A wind from the north is rustling the pines,
   Bringing a definite chill.
Splashes of scarlet and gold are the signs
   That Autumn is rounding the hill.

Leaves lose their holdings and float all around,
   Dropping knee-deep in the way;
They're making snug hideouts, softer than down,
   Where eager young children can play.

Wild geese, in formation, take off in flight,
   Yielding to radars inborn.
Orchards hang heavy, a beautiful sight,
   And Harvest is filling the horn.

Hayrides entice; happy barn dancers call;
   Smart joggers grow trim by the mile;
Bonfires are puffing the essence of fall,
   While cookouts are served family style.

Signs of the season, once scattered and new,
   Are evidenced everywhere.
God's in His Heaven, available, too,
   As close as a whispered prayer.

Alice Leedy Mason

Autumn Leaves Are Falling

Autumn is like a beautiful sunset at the end of the day, the twilight of a passing year. Nature's activities have come to fruition, and Mother Nature is about to take a well-deserved rest. The sun shines brightly, the sky is blue, the leaves are coloring, and the undisturbed fields are full of late-blooming flowers.

However, if autumn is here, can winter be far behind? Don't be dismayed. Winter is but a restful pause, a time of renewal before another great outburst of luxurious growth. If the more barren, cold season did not occur, the glorious displays of coming seasons would never develop.

As the days grow shorter, the plants undergo great changes that produce the wonderful masses of color in deciduous plants and eventually cause the leaves to fall. Shorter days cause a decrease in the plant hormone, auxin, which controls the development of the prominent green pigment, chlorophyll. As the pigment disappears with declining auxin, the leaves usually reveal colors that had been previously masked by the chlorophyll. Most often the yellow pigments carotene and xanthophyll are present, giving the leaves a yellow or yellow orange appearance. These pigments are the same compounds that give color to carrots, egg yolks and lemon rind.

The attractive red and red purple colors are the result of pigments called anthocyanins, often seen in ripe apples, tomatoes and strawberries. Two factors cause the production of these pigments: the bright sunny days and the cool nights below 45°F. Under these conditions the leaves produce a considerable amount of sugar during the day which remains partially trapped in the leaves on the cooler nights. Some of the sugar is changed into anthocyanins. Rainy, cloudy, or unusually warm nights may diminish the red colors, but the yellow and orange colors are not affected. When these red and yellow pigments are entirely lacking, the leaves usually appear brown.

There is a popular belief that frost is necessary to create leaf color. The truth is that frost may kill both the leaf cells and their pigments, causing the leaf to turn brown. The frosty nights may enhance the leaf color provided the foliage is not damaged, but it is not necessary.

During the early days of October in the northern part of the country, the first mass of color comes from the bright yellow leaves of the hickories, ashes, and poplars, and the red purple leaves of the shrubby gray dogwoods. Uniquely, the white ashes may vary from their usual bright yellow color to shades of pink and purple. Closely succeeding this display are striking masses of yellow, orange and red colors from the maples. Finally, the oaks produce a more muted mass of red and red purple leaves that remain until the first days of November.

The loss of auxin also stimulates the growth of a layer between the end of the leaf stem and the woody plant stem which eventually cuts off the leaf from the plant. This abscission layer quickly dries and becomes a brittle partition. Any pressure by wind, snow, rain, or just the weight of the leaf itself can split this partition allowing the leaf to fall to the ground without leaving any exposed wound.

The shortening days of autumn also affect the hormonal composition of many animals, thereby influencing their actions. Evidence of this is seen in the migration of the birds and the frantic food storing of the squirrels. Woodchucks, chipmunks, and ground squirrels (called gophers) are stimulated to feed heavily on the abundant plant materials resulting in a large amount of fat accumulating in their bodies. By late autumn they remain in their underground chambers and go into a deep sleep as their body functions slow to a fraction of their original tempo. In this state of hibernation, they are able to survive the severe winter season without seeking food. Such animals as the squirrels, skunks, and raccoons may temporarily hibernate when conditions become unusually severe, but they become active again in more favorable periods.

Many animals such as deer, foxes, weasels, mink, otter, mice, and shrews continue to hunt for food throughout the year. A noticeable change can be observed in the fur of these animals, which becomes thicker and often becomes more subdued in color. Whitetail deer turn from bright brown to a gray brown, and even more striking, the weasels turn from brown to a handsome white in the northern climes to match the winter snow.

Many great and wondrous changes occur in autumn that are fascinating to observe. This is the best season to appreciate nature's awesome splendor and to enjoy the peaceful transition to a time of rest.

Harold W. Rock

Framed within the casement of my window I can see—the rich and varied colors of the autumn tapestry—worked in glowing shades of red and russet, mauve and blue—the garden in the foreground and beyond—the rolling view . . .

Sunflowers blazing round the path and dahlias bold and bright—beds of gay chrysanthemums, bronze, amber, rose and white—massed against the mellow background of the distant scene—stretching to the far horizon, brown and gold and green . . .

AUTUMN TAPESTRY

Patience Strong

Furrowed acres newly ploughed, the cornstacks and the hay—orchards, stubbles, cottage roofs and churches, old and gray—meadow pastures, willow-fringed, where flow the winding streams—lovely as a picture in the tapestry of dreams.

Share Some Gold

Quietly and subtly Mother Nature goes about her yearly ritual of preparing the earth for her lovely restful season of autumn. How she must love the color of gold to use it so lavishly!

It becomes truly a golden season—with goldenrods, goldenglow, golden corn, golden pumpkins, golden apples, golden squashes, and golden grains.

Golden sunrises gleam softly through morning mists and gradually brighten to full radiance as beaming rays disperse the vapor. As day wanes, golden sunsets turn streams and lakes just a bit less golden than themselves.

Golden days glide smoothly into nights made golden by the mellow glow of the harvest moon. This softly shining moon spreads a shimmering, glimmering pathway on lakes and streams. What beauty! What serenity!

With so much gold it is almost a King Midas world, but, unlike his world where objects become motionless and lifeless, the things Mother Nature touches so lovingly become vibrantly alive and are her golden treasures of autumn.

Even rainy days wear the look of sunshine reflected from golden-leaved trees. There can be no dark, dreary days while bright leaves remain!

Maybe we could take a tip from Mother Nature and impart a glowing radiance to our surroundings. We could, you know. Smiles, like sunshine, bring a warm glow. We could share some golden moments. We could build some golden memories for ourselves and for others. We could make our days more vibrantly alive. Share some gold!

Mildred Jordan

The Letter

I found the letter the other day while I was trying once again to clean the attic. It was yellowed with age, creased from many readings, and still bore the unmistakable trace of tears shed in the reading. As I spread the letter out on my lap and started reading, I was transported back thirty years in time.

Dear Daughter,

As I start this letter to you, I am sure you are sound asleep in your own room at home. You are surrounded with all the things that have been dear to you in childhood—your stuffed animals, posters, high school trophies, and prom programs. But when you read this letter, you will be five hundred miles away in your college dormitory room. I hope you will grow to love it as you do the room in which you are now dreaming.

You are starting a whole new life now. If you do not like the image you presented in high school, you can change all that. No one knows you there. You are, in a sense, being reborn. Not everyone gets a chance to start all over. Take advantage of it if you feel the need.

You are going from a small town and a little high school to a cosmopolitan environment where many things will be new and strange. Look at each event; examine each thought. Accept those things which you feel will make you a better person and discard those which you know are only superficial and unimportant.

You will learn a lot in college. You will gain knowledge from books and from your teachers. More than this, you will learn how to live with and get along with people from all sorts of homes.

You will rub shoulders with those of different customs, ideas, religions, races. Be tolerant of their differences and learn from them all you can about the other people who live in the world with you.

As you know, I am not a very demonstrative person, and it is hard for me to tell you in words how much I love you. Let me just say that in the eighteen years I have known you, I have never had occasion to be ashamed of you in any way. You have always made your mother and me proud and happy, and we know that you will always continue to do so.

Good luck in this, your newest venture! Although you are leaving home, you will be in our thoughts and prayers daily.

Love,
Dad

In the thirty years since this letter was penned, I have written my own letter to four children going to college for the first time. I hope that my notes to them helped them as much as my dad's did me.

Winnifred Piper

October

October's changing magic upon my garden falls
With lacy, leafy patterns against the rough stone walls.
I can smell the leaves in the hedgerow,
And chrysanthemums spice the air—
Fragrance of apple orchards and seed pods everywhere.
There's a lengthening of darkness
Like a blanket that covers all,
For October, fickle maiden, is ushering in the fall.

Nellie Varnes Fultz

God's Finger Painting

Oh, glorious, beautiful autumn,
With your riot of color spread,
Green and gold and scarlet,
Underfoot and overhead,

The blue of the sky for background,
And on the horizons edge,
The colorful trees in their splendor,
Ere their leaves begin to shed,

The green of last summer's grasses
Has all been overrun
With red, white, gold, and bronze,
And purple chrysanthemum.

God dipped into His wealth of colors
And, with lavish and loving hand,
Spread a glowing finger painting
To grace our beloved land.

Marguerite Auvil McCoy

Minnie D. Klemme

October Leaves

October leaves are brightest
On blue October skies.
See how the woods are colored
By nature's timeless dyes.

Are sumacs ever brighter
Than oak leaves on the hill,
The maple leaves more scarlet,
The elms more glowing still?

October leaves are brightest,
And just before they fall,
The wind will come
   and claim them
And scatter one and all.

One of the many poems written by Minnie Klemme begins,
"There's a sign on Klemme's Corner that depicts the Oxbow Trail,
As it led across the prairies ever westward without fail . . ."
This particular verse describes the historic marker that welcomes travelers
to Murdock, Nebraska. Amid corn and wheatfields near Murdock is the
Klemme family farm, where Miss Klemme resides with her mother and a
brother. Love of good poetry has been an integral part of the Klemme
family life. Mother Klemme, a native of Germany, now ninety-four, still
recalls the German classics, poems and songs of her heritage. Minnie
Klemme has written several thousand poems in both German and English.
Listed in *Who's Who in Poetry,* she also holds memberships in Ars
Poetica and the National Society of Published Poets. Miss Klemme has
worked for several organizations throughout the United States and holds a
scholarship to Nebraska Wesleyan University. Farm chores, gardening,
and yard work take up a good portion of her time, but she enjoys writing for
a special assignment and giving poetry readings. She finds one of the most
delightful aspects of meeting people is sharing the fact that her name,
Minnie D. Klemme, means "Little Pinch of Love."

One Autumn Hour

The goldenrod is banner-bright;
Wild asters are the same.
The elderberry's beads are black;
The sumac turns to flame.

The pheasant cock is full of grain;
His challenge fills the air.
There'll be another frost tonight,
And soon the trees are bare.

The farmer harvests browning fields
To bring the corn crop home,
Ev'n as the late bee gleans for gold
To fill the honeycomb.

The field mouse lines her snug, warm nest;
The squirrel claims his tree;
And I would hold this hour in trust
For all the days to be.

September

Oh, to know the end of summer
With the corn husks getting dry,
Goldenrods in roadside splendor,
Autumn hazes in the sky.

Looking back upon the summer,
Looking forward to the fall,
With the middle of September
Is the nicest time of all.

From a Vineyard

In autumn when the grapevines
Hang heavy with purple clusters
And the air is throbbing with late bees,
There comes a day to tread the winepress,
To take the sun and make the most of these;
For winter is not long in coming,
And snow may fall before the month will close;
It's to the vineyard we are going
All up and down the jeweled rows.

And should a blue jay voice a challenge
And call us thief to his own claim,
We'll leave him yet a few green stragglers
And carry home the purple flame.

In a Golden Hour

I have seen the sunrise,
Felt its noontime heat,
Watched the sundial marking
Every hour complete.

Now I see the sunrise
In a golden hour,
See its rays far-reaching,
Bright and filled with power.

Know as day is ending,
Life goes ever on,
Even as the sunsets
On tomorrow's dawn.

Of Red and Brown

Now in the waterways along the milo fields
The deer blend perfectly with the red brown
Heads of ripened grain.

Motion gives them away,
As two pairs of hooves clear the ravine,
Followed by two pairs more.

Beautiful, beautiful autumn—
Lately green and gold, copper and bronze,
Soon to be all brown again—
Till the wind shifts, and the snow drifts
Over the fields and meadows and woodland,
And the world awakens to a white countryside
Where red brown deer
Leave little hoof marks
In the white and beautiful snow.

The Harvesters

There was a time when grain shocks graced the fields,
When binders cut the grain and bound the sheaves,
When wheat and oats and rye and barley yields
Made work from many dawns to many eves.
And centuries before, man cut the grain
With sickle in the hand and bound the same;
And gleaners followed after, gleaned again
Against the time when famine made its claim.
I never see a field of growing wheat,
But that I know that here is bread to eat.
I never see the combines, strange machines,
But that I know man harvests yet and gleans,
That here is work which still brings man his food;
And knowing this, I own that God is good.

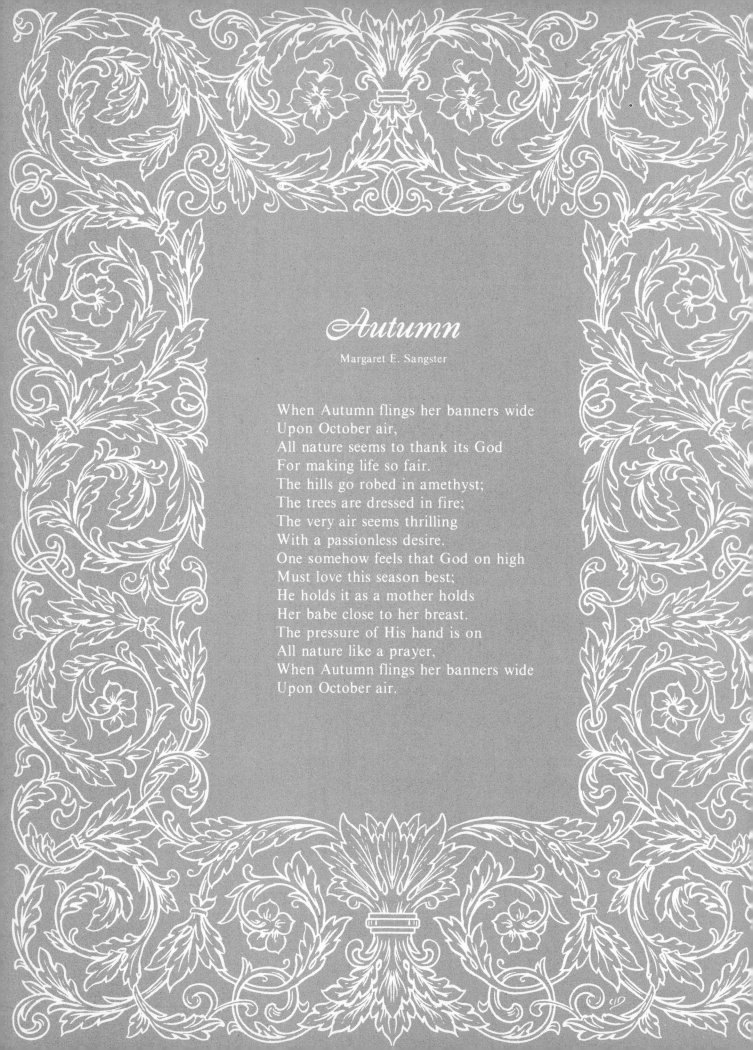

Autumn

Margaret E. Sangster

When Autumn flings her banners wide
Upon October air,
All nature seems to thank its God
For making life so fair.
The hills go robed in amethyst;
The trees are dressed in fire;
The very air seems thrilling
With a passionless desire.
One somehow feels that God on high
Must love this season best;
He holds it as a mother holds
Her babe close to her breast.
The pressure of His hand is on
All nature like a prayer,
When Autumn flings her banners wide
Upon October air.

Grandmother's Button Jar

It stands on the window shelf above my typewriter, next to the ceramic pot that holds my pencils and pens: a four-ounce clear glass jar that once held shapeless coffee granules. It's jammed with buttons of all shapes and sizes, each circle or square, each color a memory to warm the spirit.

I spill the contents in the sunlight onto my desk; as I spread and finger them, the buttons come to life. Each tells a story of my grandmother's marriage.

Carefully I turn the small delicate china pansy that my grandmother, after much searching, finally ordered from the catalog at the general store. The button matched the fabric of the dress she sewed for her first meeting with the man she would later marry.

At the Harvest Dance, when they were introduced, he said, "They match your eyes, those pretty flowers," and the warmth in his voice made her blush.

As I move the buttons on my desk, a tiny pearl glistens in the bright light. It was one of the closely spaced fastenings that trickled down the lace jacket of the wedding dress she fashioned and then stitched by hand because the fabric was too fragile to trust to her sewing machine.

There are from that jar many pale wee creatures in pastels. They fastened baby sweaters she knitted for each child as their family and their love grew.

She showed me each wooden button and described the sweaters and jackets they helped hold tight about small children; buttons bulky enough so that awkward little hands could manage them.

And, as the children grew, there were buttons of favorite colors to match the dresses she stitched throughout the years, because money was not plentiful, and her love gave her strength for the labor which she called her "creativity time."

My mother remembers how her mother sat at that sewing machine with children playing on the floor around her. In time, Grandfather bought her an electric machine, and she could speed through seams endlessly, it seemed, without tiring.

And one Easter, when she had sewn matching dresses in navy blue with bright red and white buttons marching down to their waists for all my aunts, photographers waiting at the town church to photograph the Easter Parade paid more attention to her family than they did to the local celebrities.

When many of her friends could afford furs, Grandmother knitted a full-length cape to wear to a town function. It resembled the skin of a mink, and she adorned it with amber buttons that perfectly matched the tint of the wool. She was the center of attention, winning the admiration of both men and women. And Granddad beamed at the compliments paid to her.

Each button in that jar had a place in her heart and in her memory, and she saved them carefully through the years, one button for each important event in her life.

I fondle the buttons and carefully place them back in the jar.

The last button is a brilliant crystal centered in lustrous onyx. It secured about her the mourning suit she sewed with trembling hands the week Grandfather waited for death. The sparkle of the button fulfilled a wish he had expressed that "you won't become a dull colorless woman after I've gone."

Sometime later she gave me the button jar. It's mine to pass on to my daughter, so she'll know the story of her great-grandmother.

I turn my grandmother's button jar on the shelf so that the sun will warm all the symbols of her life—so they'll come alive in its rays, bouncing sunlight into my eyes and keeping bright memories of my grandmother.

Naomi Cherkofsky

What Is a Flower?

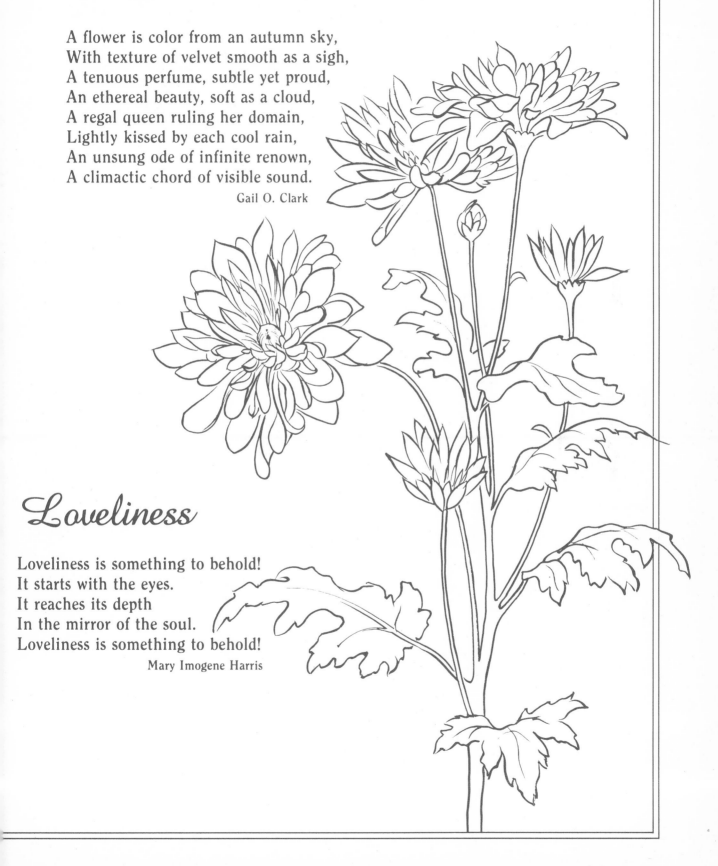

A flower is color from an autumn sky,
With texture of velvet smooth as a sigh,
A tenuous perfume, subtle yet proud,
An ethereal beauty, soft as a cloud,
A regal queen ruling her domain,
Lightly kissed by each cool rain,
An unsung ode of infinite renown,
A climactic chord of visible sound.

Gail O. Clark

Loveliness

Loveliness is something to behold!
It starts with the eyes.
It reaches its depth
In the mirror of the soul.
Loveliness is something to behold!

Mary Imogene Harris

Discovering Autumn's Wild Fruits

Michele Arrieh

Although some people consider autumn a melancholy time of year with its withered flowers and fallen leaves, others delight in the plentiful array of ripened wild fruits the season brings. Field and forest yield succulent berries, seeds and nuts in endless variety, providing man with unusual taste treats and animals with their winter food supply.

Throughout the centuries, man has enjoyed feasting on nature's autumnal offerings. As long ago as 2400 B.C., grapes were a popular fruit in Egypt. They are the first cultivated food mentioned in the Bible and were an important monetary crop to the Romans.

Wild fruits were an indispensable source of food for the American Indians and were also employed for healing purposes. Varieties of wild berries, nuts and seeds were a major part of their diet and were stored for use during long cold winters when rations dwindled. Acorns and sunflower seeds were especially used by Indians who ate them raw or roasted and ground them to thicken stews and flavor breads.

The early American settlers found many uses for wild fruits, baking them in pies, breads and cakes and sealing them as tangy jellies and jams for later use. The dyeing qualities of many berries were not overlooked for use as ink and lip rouge. The colonists also discovered that they could obtain dark stains by boiling the husks of various nuts.

It is impossible to know how many species of berries grow in the world, since they are constantly changing by natural mutation. Some berries have existed from earliest history, such as the hearty elderberry, which is still used today as in Roman times for wine. These berries also assure exceptional pies, pastries and preserves.

Besides the dozen or so blueberry varieties already in cultivation, there are more than fifty types growing in the wilds. The native blueberries thrive in many locations from wetlands to medium dry lands, at the edges of woods or in the open countryside, on hilltops or mountainsides, and in many places in between.

Another equally prevalent berry is the huckleberry. Its exceptionally beautiful shrub has dainty oval leaves and delicate grayish brown branches that bear sprays of the shiny black berries. Huckleberries make delicious pies and are also tasty served fresh with whipped cream.

The berries of the wild currant are smooth, red, firm and sour. The Indians found many ways to enjoy this versatile fruit, and soon the early American settlers also discovered the currant's value for baking, beverages, and especially for its delicious jelly. Currants were often dried for use in the winter.

So many varieties of blackberries exist that it is impossible even for plant experts to number them. Popular strains resulting from cultivated and natural crossing include loganberries, boysenberries and dewberries, each having a distinctive flavor, but all excellent for baking and cooking.

Other fruits of autumn include wild nuts which swell on branches in profuse clusters, ripen and fall to the ground as freely as the colorful leaves that shaded them.

Especially abundant and widespread are black walnuts which have shells that are encased in soft husks. The early settlers and Indians spread these freshly gathered nuts in the sun until they were partially dried, which made separating the husks from the shells easier. The nuts would also lose some of their inherent bitterness during this natural drying process.

The early settlers also learned from the Indians how to use both the sap and fruit of the butternut tree. The butternut shell is very hard and rough, but once it is broken, the kernel separates easily and is very sweet and delicious.

Hickory nuts require little effort to harvest, since they fall to the ground already husked. Many people consider these nuts the finest of wild varieties. The pecan, one species of hickory that is well-known and appreciated, is excellent for eating raw and for use in baking.

Another wild nut that cannot be overlooked is the hazelnut which grows on small bushes along many roadsides. Although these round, sweet little nuts ripen in late August, they usually cling to their branches until the end of fall. They are easily shelled and a pleasure to eat.

If you observe the seasonal changes, autumn provides an opportunity to discover some of nature's finest treasures. This is the time when summer's blossoms are fulfilled, reaching their fruition in the bountiful ripening of autumn fruits.

Apricot Nut Bars

Makes 12 to 16 bars.

¾ cup dried apricots (or other dried fruit: raisins, prunes, dates, peaches)

Shortbread

1 cup whole wheat pastry flour
¼ cup brown sugar, firmly packed
¼ cup wheat germ
½ cup butter or margarine

Put apricots in a small pan and cover with water. Over medium heat, cook, covered, until tender. Drain (keep juice for other purpose), cool, and chop into small pieces.

Preheat oven to 325°. In a small bowl, mix together flour, brown sugar, and wheat germ. Cut in butter with a pastry blender until mixture resembles crumbs. Pat into a 9-inch square baking pan and bake 25 minutes or until lightly browned.

Spread Topping over hot, baked layer and put in oven again for about 35 minutes or until toothpick inserted in center comes out clean. Cool in pan before slicing into bars.

Topping

2 eggs, well beaten
1 cup firmly packed brown sugar
  the prepared fruit
½ teaspoon baking powder
⅓ cup whole wheat flour
½ teaspoon salt
½ teaspoon vanilla
½ cup chopped walnuts

Combine eggs and brown sugar. Stir in the prepared fruit and remaining ingredients.

Honey-Nut Balls

Makes approximately 1½ dozen.

½ cup peanut butter
¼ cup honey
½ cup or more non-instant powdered milk or soy milk powder
1 tablespoon sunflower seed
1 tablespoon chopped walnuts
1 tablespoon raisins or currants
3 tablespoons sesame seed

Mix peanut butter and honey until well blended. Gradually add powdered milk until mixture resembles bread dough. Stir in remaining ingredients, except sesame seed. If more fruit or nuts are desired, add to taste. Roll mixture into small balls and roll in the sesame seed. Refrigerate until needed.

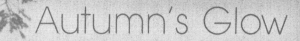

Autumn's Glow

Goldenrod and purple asters
Fill each little wayside nook;
Queen Anne's lace and scarlet sumac
Gaily nod beside the brook.

Blue mist clings about the mountain;
Crystal-clear the lake below
Mirrors panoramic beauty,
Softly etched in autumn's glow.

Caroline H. Bair

Tranquillity

The lake shone like a looking glass
So placid and serene;
Solemnity was here defined—
'Twas such a peaceful scene.

The time was autumn; distant hills
Were flaming in attire;
Reflected on its surface,
They had set the lake afire!

I dropped a single pebble in
The mirrored depths, and then
When every ripple reached the shore,
Peace was restored again!

So here I stood upon the brink
Of summer and the fall
Enjoying its tranquillity
And the wonder of it all!

Georgia B. Adams

Somewhere afar in the heavens blue
Soft as the morning mist,
God sends an autumn sunbeam through
A leaf that the angels kissed,
A million shades of gold and red
Painted in splendor bright,
The silver raindrops of afternoon,
The moonlight magic of night.

Somewhere away there's a little stream
Humming a merry tune,
Sparkling and fair in a lonely spot
Under an autumn moon;
This is October, pleasant and gay
Charmed by the summer's end—
These things make autumn all that it is
With so many dreams she can lend.

Somewhere, a whisper, a soft gentle breeze
Thrilling our hearts with its song,
Somewhere, a hope and a faith unsurpassed,
Part of this heavenly dawn,
Dear Mother Nature, paint brush in hand,
Her masterpiece, gold against blue,
Everywhere beauties your mind can enjoy—
These things make autumn for you.

These Things
Make Autumn

Garnett Ann Schultz

Destiny

I have listened to your whisper,
And I never yet could learn
What it is you're always lisping
As you creep among the ferns.

I have watched you rolling onward
Where the great gray rocks intrude
And heard you loudly murmur
Through the dark and solemn woods.

Green mosses there are drinking
From your overflowing stream,
And the wild flower bending meekly
Inhales thy breath unseen.

Yet heedless of wily tempters
That long to have you stay,
You onward rush unheeding,
Following the marked out way.

Till on some beetling cliff
By subtle magic stayed,
You pause—in fear to leap
Down the rugged path that's laid.

Henrietta Peck

The War of the Worlds Broadcast

Halloween has always been a time for mischief makers, but it seems they had their heyday in the 1930s. Young pranksters hit the streets causing local havoc. City youngsters soaped windows and rang doorbells, while their country cousins overturned outhouses and reassembled wagons atop farm sheds. And on the evening of October 30, 1938, a prankster by the name of Orson Welles hit the airwaves causing nationwide hysteria.

Between eight and nine o'clock (EST), while half of the radio audience was laughing at Charlie McCarthy, other listeners were being scared out of their homes. In a radio dramatization of H.G. Wells' "The War of the Worlds," Orson Welles and the Mercury Theatre on the Air presented a fantasy about an invasion from Mars. The program led thousands in the home audience to believe the planet Earth was actually being invaded by Martians. The confusion was regrettable, but real.

The program began with a weather report, followed by dance music which was interrupted by an announcement concerning explosions of gas on the planet Mars. The music resumed only to be interrupted again and again by special bulletins about a meteor that landed near Grovers Mill, New Jersey. Further break-ins brought alarming information—it had not been a meteor but a metal cylinder containing monsters armed with death rays. The broadcast included interviews with an astronomer from the nearby Princeton Observa-

tory and on-the-spot reports from terrified spectators. Amid the discourse of death and destruction, an official-sounding voice told the nation to remain calm. But, what was intended to be a Halloween prank became a Halloween panic.

Projected in the form of news bulletins, the authenticity of the attack seemed unquestionable to many. As the actors' voices continued to relate eyewitness details of the invasion, radio listeners overloaded the telephone lines with frantic calls to the police, newspapers, and radio stations. Those who had come to believe the fiction was fact fled to their cars and jammed the highways hoping to find an escape from the devastation. Complete chaos hit towns like Newark where families rushed out of their homes holding handkerchiefs over their faces to protect themselves from Martian gases. If they had only known the landing site had been selected by a playwright making a pencil mark on a New Jersey map!

The program was announced as a play at the beginning and interrupted three times for similar announcements to reassure the audience. Nevertheless, scores of people found it possible to believe that Martians had landed on Earth, demolished the United States army, occupied most of the country, and were eventually destroyed by bacteria, all within the span of forty-five minutes! It was such an absurd incident that the resulting public panic could not have been predicted, not even by Orson Welles. At the age of twenty-three,

Welles not only starred in the show, but instigated and directed the event. However, this is not to hold him responsible for the explosive result.

Perhaps if the incident had not occurred during the precarious years leading to World War II, the public would have taken what they heard more lightly. Switching the radio dial to another station would have dispelled the illusion of a world catastrophe. But in a troubled world, much of the everyday news was unsettling and often seemed unbelievable. Americans had already been shocked by the stock market crash and the Depression. A populace already nervous with the threat of war and disaster was prepared to believe the worst. Submerged fears surfaced quickly during that anxious period. Some citizens even assumed the invasion was a camouflage under which the Germans were attacking. Professor Hadley Cantril of Princeton made a study and estimated that over one million of the six million listeners took the broadcast literally and reacted "according to their natures."

Announcements stating that the broadcast was only a play continued throughout the evening. But a highly tense audience had already suffered the effect of too much dramatic realism. Not until dawn had the entire nation finally quieted down. The following morning, newspaper headlines echoed the atmosphere of terror that reigned the night before. For days, articles told of the madness that had swept the country and related the repercussions of the episode.

Fortunately no one died in the mass panic, but many accidents were reported, and a man in Pittsburgh found his wife about to take poison. Individuals injured in the scramble to escape viewed those responsible for the broadcast as villains. Outraged citizens threatened lawsuits. Hundreds of complaints poured into the Federal Communications Commission and the Columbia Broadcasting System (CBS), the network that aired the broadcast, which resulted in a strong recommendation that future simulated news broadcasts were to be avoided. The issue of government censorship and increased control of radio was discussed and dismissed, because harmful propaganda could be issued by controlled sources. The event clearly demonstrated radio's impact and the power of suggestion through the mass media.

A radio station in Lima, Peru, broadcast the play in Spanish a year later. This program also caused a panic which resulted in irate Peruvians burning down the station. Wisconsin-born Orson Welles ultimately fared much better with his production. Public opinion reversed itself after the excitement died down. A Milwaukee newspaper received calls praising the program, saying it was thrilling and there should be more like it. Welles and his cast were considered heroes by columnists who felt they had alerted the country by showing how vulnerable it was to panic in the event of war.

Orson Welles became a world celebrity overnight. He soon took his players from the Mercury Theatre on the Air to Hollywood for another controversial production, "Citizen Kane." His depiction of William Randolph Hearst in the film caused him more problems in California than his radio show had in New York. But, coast to coast, that prankster would always be remembered most for his Halloween broadcast of "The War of the Worlds," the most famous dramatic broadcast of all time. As Orson said at the end of the program, it was "the Mercury Theatre's own radio version of dressing up in a sheet and jumping out of a bush and saying 'Boo'!"

Gale Wiersum Clapper

Autumn Glory

While walking in the woods today,
I marveled at the bright array
  Of Autumn robes the trees had donned.
  How blue the tranquil sky beyond!
Could this be real—this fairyland
Of red and gold? And there I'd stand
  Enraptured—far as eye could see—
  At Mother Nature's artistry.

The maples wore rich gold brocade;
The oaks wore red; the balsams jade;
  The stately elms in jasmine dressed,
  As did the willows; and the rest
Were garbed in splendor, one and all,
For their majestic Harvest Ball.
  And, underneath, in their cool shade,
  Wild asters, ferns and gentians played.

In verdant meadows, goldenrods
Were gently swaying; milkweed pods
  Were sending forth their snowy down,
  As cattails shed their coats of brown.
Long rows of sumac, crimson-dyed,
Had set aflame the whole hillside.
  Above wild geese in southward flight,
  October's sun shone warm and bright.

Then sunset came; a velvet sky
Was tinted with a scarlet dye.
  And o'er this red and gold and green
  There came a stillness so serene,
As if all nature bowed its head
In worship; then I knew who spread
  This crown of glory o'er the land;
  It was the Master's loving hand.

Helen D. Hering

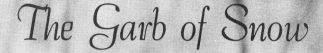

The Garb of Snow

I watched God clothe the world last night
With snowflake crystals clean and white;
This morning every barren tree
Was beautiful as it could be.

The field that looked so bare and brown
This morning has a snow-white gown,
And pine trees laden full of snow
Are lovely in the sunlight's glow.

The fenceposts, too, are painted white
With snow that fell and froze last night,
And o'er it all the sunlight gleams
In beauty far beyond our dreams.

Such loveliness o'er all the land
Is painted by the Master's hand,
And we can only stand and gaze
With hearts o'erflowing with His praise.

Hazel Rugg

What Better Place?

Mary A. Selden

When Indian summer comes to the farm,
   What better place can there be
For Halloween spirits to congregate
   In eerie company?

Corn shocks in the wide north field
   Are marching row on row;
Owls glide, and witches ride
   When the moon begins to glow.

Pumpkins line the front porch steps
   And grin through the windowpane;
Our old black cat with her yellow eyes
   Must sing a weird refrain.

Goblins, wailing "trick or treat,"
   Are invited to come inside
For cider and doughnuts and apples on sticks,
   While we look on wide-eyed.

When Indian summer comes to the farm,
   Country girls and boys
Look ahead to an evening of Halloween fun
   With all its childhood joys.

Halloween

Ruth Hathaway Miller

Corn shocks and pumpkins,
　Cider nice and sweet,
Doughnuts and apples,
　All that one can eat.

Funny masks and costumes,
　Children playing pranks,
Wildly ringing doorbells,
　Irritated cranks,

Skeletons a-dancing,
　A big October moon,
Ugly-looking witches
　Riding on a broom,

Bats and ghosts and goblins;
　Black cats, horns and owls;
Weird bewitching magic;
　Eerie shrieks and howls;

Laughing jack-o'-lanterns,
　Funniest ever seen,
Children all so happy
　'Cause it's Halloween.

Interstice

Nature, in her rhythms, sets a time for all things. In the yearly cycle of seasons she bestows a time for planting, a time for growing, a time for reaping and a time for rest and renewal.

Each season is a cup full to the brim and running over with its particular joys and pleasures: the green promises of spring, the golden growth of summer, fall's bursts of glorious colors, the icy tingles mixed with the cozy warmth of winter. Each season is glutted with riches so full that endless partaking would benumb the tasting of them.

So, wisely, Nature limits the seasons. And in between them, she tucks an in-between time, an interval, an interstice. This "small or narrow space" signals the end of one season and the anticipation of another.

Between Fall and Winter the interstitial cup refills itself daily with new delights. The balmy days of October's Indian summer, with trees rioting in their last colorful fling, linger on memory's tongue like a sip of rare wine, delicate and fleeting.

Each day, each night, each hour and minute flow quickly one after the other, each different, more beautiful, more fragile than the one before. And the present becomes more precious because it soon will be the past.

The leaves fall, rustling to join in brown bands around tree trunks, skittering across the back roads and country lanes, dappling the pools of creeks and streams.

The daily arc of the sun, headed toward its winter solstice, flattens, and the day's allotment of sunlight dwindles. The sun sinks blood-red, blackening bare branches. The wind swings to the north, and the morning dawns with a bite in the air.

Winter hovers around the corner. An early snow, soft and clingy, a precursor of storms to come, stirs man and beast to prepare.

Nature only slowly makes or allows changes. But in her seasons she compasses the slow rhythm of change to show us the wholeness of life. And in between comes the time to reflect on and to savor the past, and to prepare for and ponder the future.

Interstice—in a time for all things, a time sweetened by its brevity beyond its duration.

Bill Nunn

ACKNOWLEDGMENTS

A LABOR DAY GIFT by Carole Joyce Davis. Courtesy SUNSHINE MAGAZINE. SEPTEMBER by Emilee Hines. Reprinted with permission from FARM WIFE NEWS, P. O. Box 643, Milwaukee, WI 53201. TIME BENDS THE BOUGH by Fern M. Impola. From WE OF THE NORTH by Fern M. Impola. Used with permission. THE HARVEST'S GOLDEN BEAUTY . . . by Elizabeth Searle Lamb. From the selection THE GOLDEN HARVEST, taken from the book TODAY AND EVERY DAY by Elizabeth Searle Lamb, Copyright © 1970 by Unity School of Christianity. HALLOWEEN by Ruth Hathaway Miller. From her book JUST EVERYDAY POEMS, Copyright © 1952 by Ruth Hathaway Miller. THE LETTER by Winnifred E. Piper. Used with permission of the author. AUTUMN LAUGHTER by Annette Wildman Swearingen. From her book OF HEART AND HOME. Used with permission. Recipes for: APRICOT NUT BARS and HONEY-NUT BALLS from IDEALS NATURALLY NUTRITIOUS COOKBOOK by Donna M. Paananen, Copyright © 1978 by Ideals Publishing Corporation. Our sincere thanks to the following authors whose addresses we were unable to locate: Ruth Winslow Gordon for AUTUMN'S COMING; Henrietta Peck for DESTINY (originally titled MY BROOK); Harmony Schupp for SEPTEMBER.

COLOR ART AND PHOTO CREDITS
(in order of appearance)

Front and back covers, Lake Michigamme, Marquette County, Michigan, Ken Dequaine; inside front and back covers, AUTUMN LANDSCAPE, R. Lardinois; Colorado River at Lees Ferry, Arizona, Ed Cooper; Country lane, Barnet, Vermont, Alpha Photo Associates; A stroll through the leaves, Robert E. Hamilton; Grapes and goldenrod, Gerald Koser; FALL IN THE COUNTRY, Otto Modersohn, Three Lions, Inc.; Wheatfield, H. Armstrong Roberts; Hillside pasture, Barnet, Vermont, Fred Sieb; Autumn village, East Topsham, Vermont, Freelance Photographers Guild; Church in the valley, East Topsham, Vermont, Fred Sieb; Autumn arrangement, Fred Sieb; Fruits of harvest, Fred Sieb; Exploring in the fall, Bob Taylor; Hatch Pond, East Madison, New Hampshire, Fred Sieb; Colorful display, Peter C. Aitken; Friendly street, Tamworth, New Hampshire, Fred Sieb; Woodland garden, Fred Sieb; ON THE TERRACE, Pierre Auguste Renoir, Three Lions, Inc.; Autumn flowers, Gerald Koser; Autumn reflections, Moose Pond, Maine, Fred Sieb; Playful stream, Fred Sieb; Middle Genessee Falls, Letchworth State Park, New York, Ed Cooper; Wanderer's paradise, H. Armstrong Roberts; Colorful walkway, Colchester, Connecticut, Fred Dole; Snow on leaves, Fred Dole; First snow, Intervale, New Hampshire, Fred Sieb.

A time for Thanksgiving ...

Join us in a rich, glorious tribute to our heritage in Thanksgiving Ideals. Splendid color photography accompanies poignant prose and poetry reflecting on the many blessings for which we give thanks.

"Thanksgiving Tapestry" features a special selection of quotes on the meaning of our first American holiday. A "Harvest Hymn," composed for Thanksgiving Day, is complemented by a Currier and Ives print, "American Homestead Autumn." Edith Shaw Butler, our featured poet, offers a touching selection of thoughts on this season of praise and thanksgiving.

Let this beautiful issue be the first in a series of keepsake volumes. Subscribe to Ideals today! Share the richness and beauty of our land with a special friend or relative. Let Ideals say, "I'm thinking of you" all year long!